OUR FAMILY TREE BIBLE

JANUARY 3, 2019
BETTY MATTESON RHODES

Our Family Tree Bible

by Betty Matteson Rhodes

Published for

Betmatrho Publications

January 3, 2019

ISBN: 9780359329878

ISBN: 978-0-359-32987-8

Printed by: Lulu.com

My Name: _____

My Birthday: _____

Where I was born: _____

My Parents names:

Father: _____   **Mother:** _____

Spouse's Name: _____ **Marriage Date:** _____

Parent(s) of my Children: (if more than one)

_____

My / Our Children:

1. _____ Date Born: _____

2. _____ Date Born: _____

3. _____ Date Born: _____

4. _____ Date Born: _____

5. _____ Date Born: _____

6. _____ Date Born: _____

7. _____ Date Born: _____

8. _____ Date Born: _____

My Spouse's Name:

_____

Spouse's Birthday:

_____

Where he/she was born:

_____

Spouse's Parent's names:

    Father: _____

    Mother: _____

  Additional Spouse of father: _____

  Additional Spouse of mother: _____

Siblings of my Spouse:

1. _____ **Date Born:** _____

2. _____ **Date Born:** _____

3. _____ **Date Born:** _____

4. _____ **Date Born:** _____

5. _____ **Date Born:** _____

6. _____ **Date Born:** _____

7. _____ **Date Born:** _____

8. _____ **Date Born:** _____

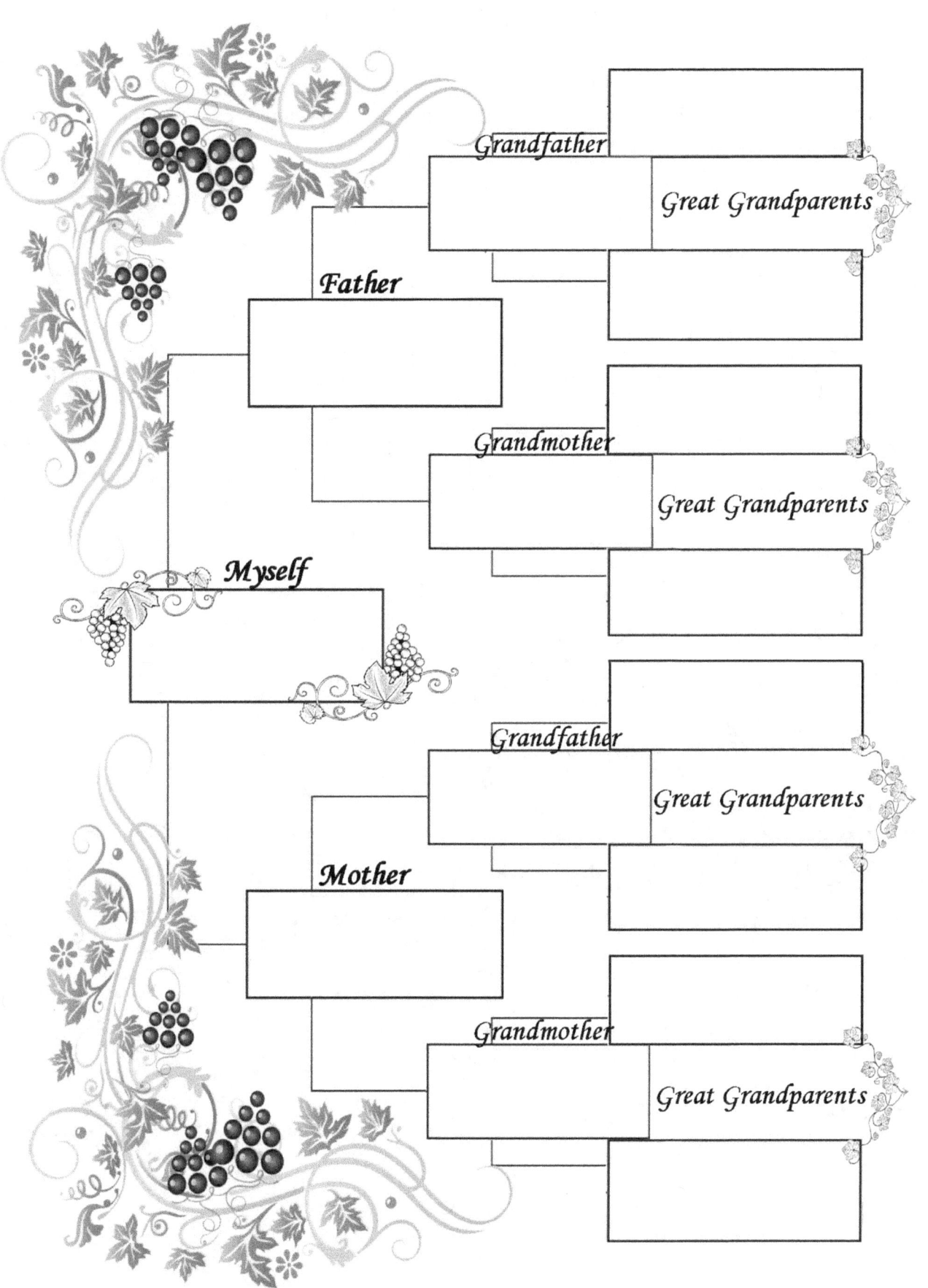

Grandfather

Great Grandparents

Father

Grandmother

Great Grandparents

Myself

Grandfather

Great Grandparents

Mother

Grandmother

Great Grandparents

My Family's Surnames

Four generations of ancestors will, in most cases, give you 16 different surnames. Fill in one surname per shield. Using only the last name, begin with your father's line on the top two rows of shields and the bottom two rows for your mother's family names. Names should be written/printed across the middle of the shields.

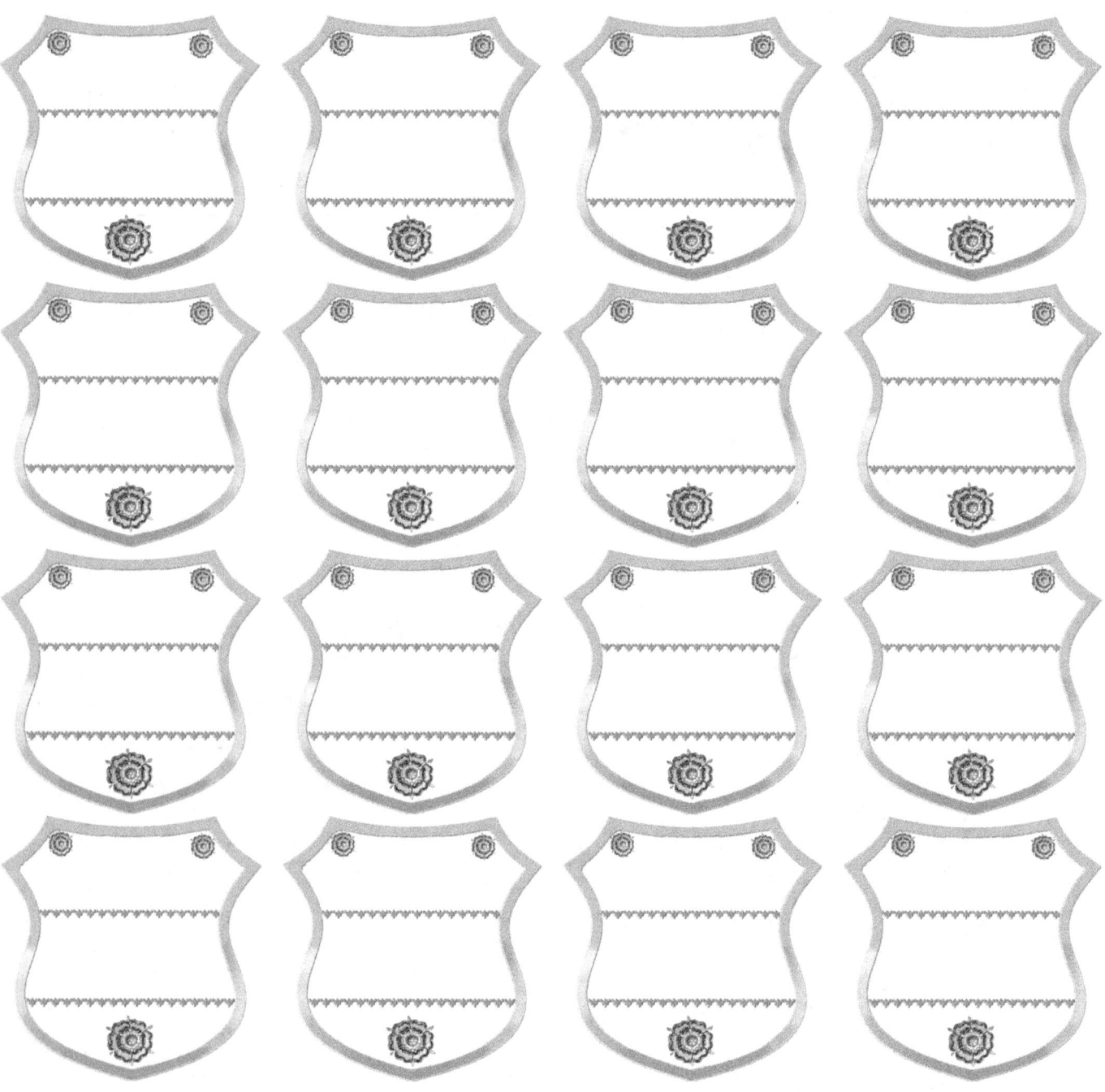

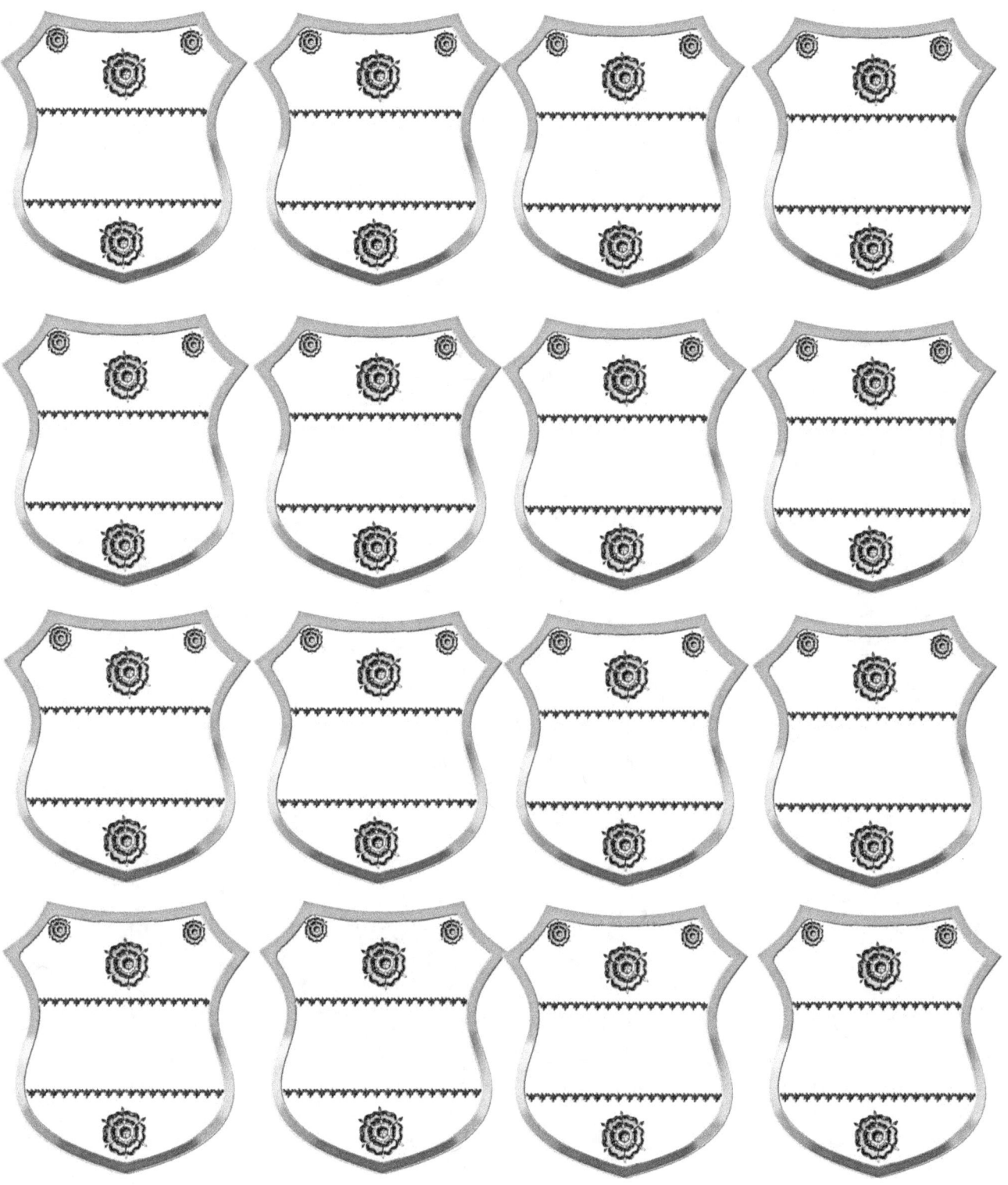

Our Family Photo

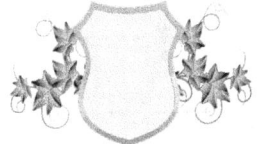

My Father's Name: _____

Father's Birthday: _____

Where he was born: _____

Date he married my Mother: _____ **Place:** _____

Father's Parent's names:

Father: _____

Mother: _____

Additional Spouse of father: _____

Additional Spouse of mother: _____

Siblings of my Father (my Aunts & Uncles):

9. _____ **Date Born:** _____

10._____ **Date Born:** _____

11._____ **Date Born:** _____

12._____ **Date Born:** _____

13._____ **Date Born:** _____

14._____ **Date Born:** _____

15._____ **Date Born:** _____

16._____ **Date Born:** _____

My Mother's Name: _____

Mother's Birthday: _____

Where She was born: _____

Date she married my Father: _____ Place: _____

Mother's Parent's names:

Father: _____

Mother: _____

Additional Spouse of her father: _____

Additional Spouse of her mother: _____

Siblings of my Mother (my Aunts & Uncles):

1. _____ Date Born: _____

2. _____ Date Born: _____

3. _____ Date Born: _____

4. _____ Date Born: _____

5. _____ Date Born: _____

6. _____ Date Born: _____

7. _____ Date Born: _____

8. _____ Date Born: _____

PATERNAL GRANDFATHER

Grandfather's Name: _____

His Birthday: _____

Where Grandpa was born: _____

Date he married Grandmother: _____ **Place:** _____

Grandpa's Parents names:

Father: _____

Mother: _____

Additional Spouse of his father: _____

Additional Spouse of his mother: _____

Grandpa's Children (My Great Aunts & Uncles)

1. _____ **Date Born:** _____

2. _____ **Date Born:** _____

3. _____ **Date Born:** _____

4. _____ **Date Born:** _____

5. _____ **Date Born:** _____

6. _____ **Date Born:** _____

7. _____ **Date Born:** _____

8. _____ **Date Born:** _____

PATERNAL GRANDMOTHER

Grandmother's Name: _____

Her Birthday: _____

Where Grandma was born: _____

Date she married Grandfather: _____ **Place:** _____

Grandma's Parents names:

Father: _____

Mother: _____

Additional Spouse of her father: _____

Additional Spouse of her mother: _____

Grandma's Children (My Great Aunts & Uncles)

1. _____ **Date Born:** _____

2. _____ **Date Born:** _____

3. _____ **Date Born:** _____

4. _____ **Date Born:** _____

5. _____ **Date Born:** _____

6. _____ **Date Born:** _____

7. _____ **Date Born:** _____

8. _____ **Date Born:** _____

MATERNAL GRANDFATHER

Grandfather's Name: _____

His Birthday: _____

Where Grandpa was born: _____

Date he married Grandmother: _____ Place: _____

Grandpa's Parents names:

Father: _____

Mother: _____

Additional Spouse of his father: _____

Additional Spouse of his mother: _____

Grandpa's Children (My Great Aunts & Uncles)

9. _____ Date Born: _____

10. _____ Date Born: _____

11. _____ Date Born: _____

12. _____ Date Born: _____

13. _____ Date Born: _____

14. _____ Date Born: _____

15. _____ Date Born: _____

16. _____ Date Born: _____

MATERNAL GRANDMOTHER

Grandmother's Name: _____

Her Birthday: _____

Where Grandma was born: _____

Date she married Grandmother: _____ Place: _____

Grandma's Parents names:

Father: _____

Mother: _____

Additional Spouse of her father: _____

Additional Spouse of her mother: _____

Grandma's Children (My Great Aunts & Great Uncles)

9. _____ Date Born: _____

10. _____ Date Born: _____

11. _____ Date Born: _____

12. _____ Date Born: _____

13. _____ Date Born: _____

14. _____ Date Born: _____

15. _____ Date Born: _____

16. _____ Date Born: _____

Paternal Grandfather's Ancestors

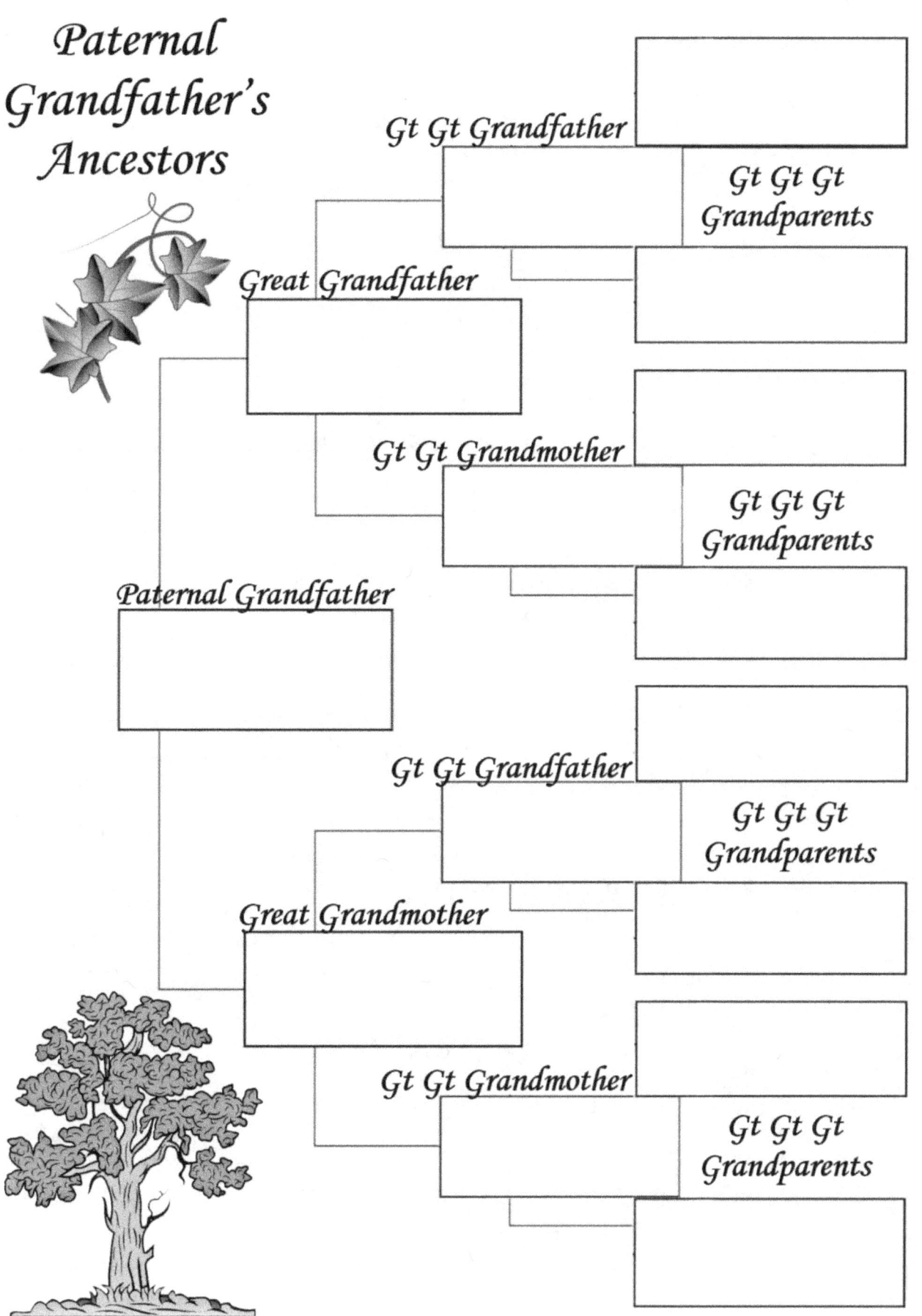

Gt Gt Grandfather

Gt Gt Gt Grandparents

Great Grandfather

Gt Gt Grandmother

Gt Gt Gt Grandparents

Paternal Grandfather

Gt Gt Grandfather

Gt Gt Gt Grandparents

Great Grandmother

Gt Gt Grandmother

Gt Gt Gt Grandparents

Paternal Grandmother's Ancestors

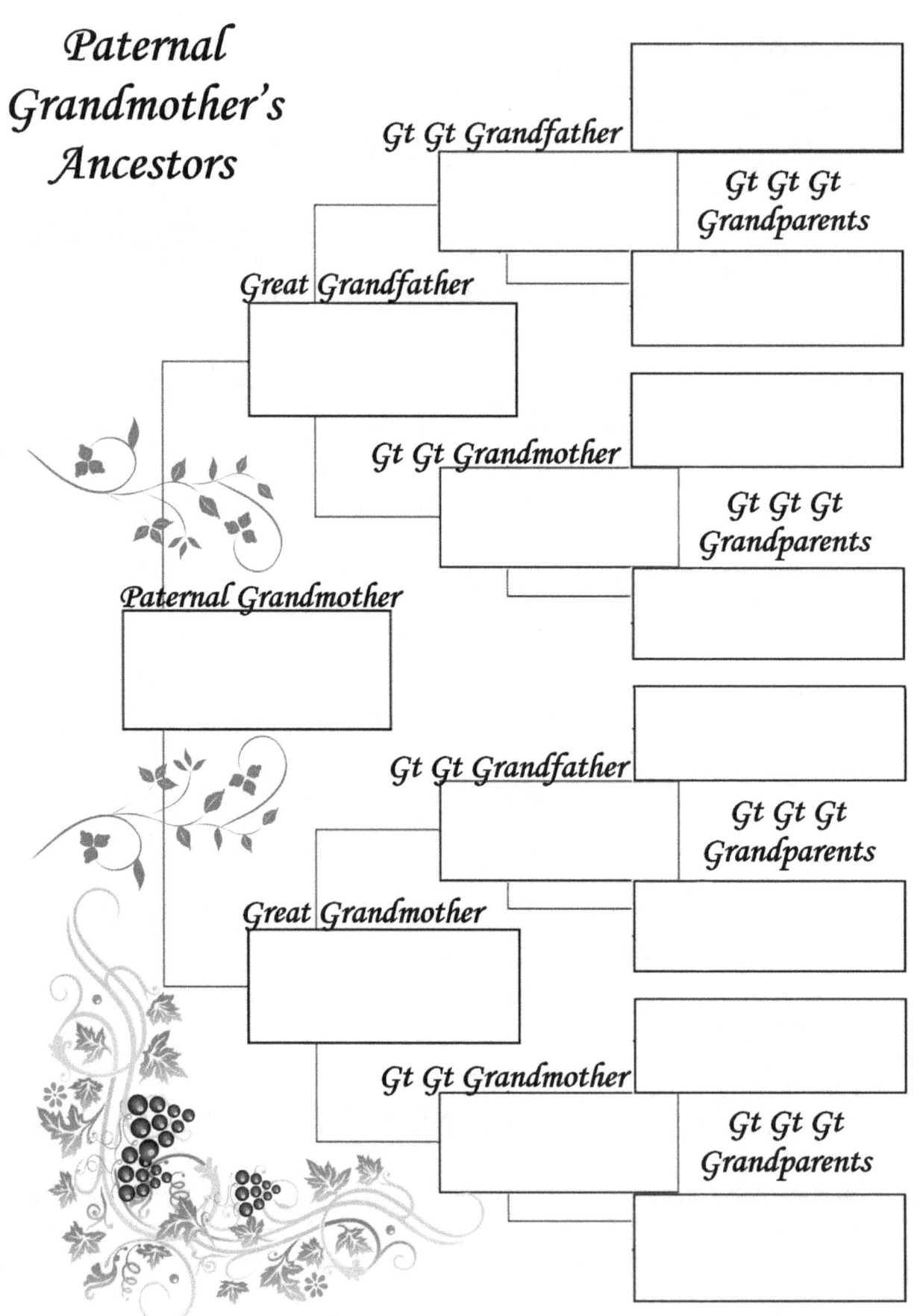

Gt Gt Grandfather

Gt Gt Gt Grandparents

Great Grandfather

Gt Gt Grandmother

Gt Gt Gt Grandparents

Paternal Grandmother

Gt Gt Grandfather

Gt Gt Gt Grandparents

Great Grandmother

Gt Gt Grandmother

Gt Gt Gt Grandparents

Maternal Grandfather's Ancestors

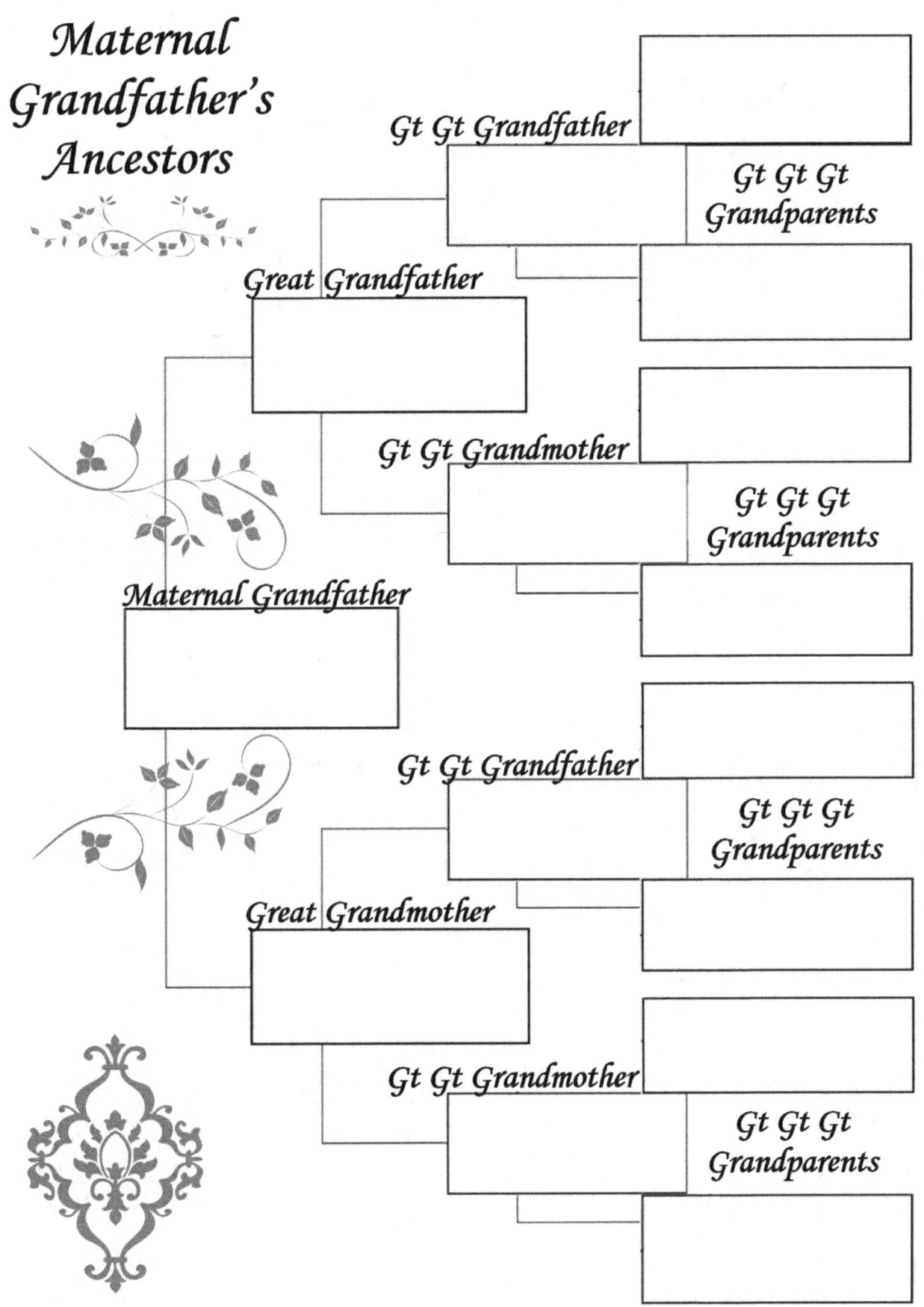

Gt Gt Grandfather

Gt Gt Gt Grandparents

Great Grandfather

Gt Gt Grandmother

Gt Gt Gt Grandparents

Maternal Grandfather

Gt Gt Grandfather

Gt Gt Gt Grandparents

Great Grandmother

Gt Gt Grandmother

Gt Gt Gt Grandparents

Maternal Grandmother's Ancestors

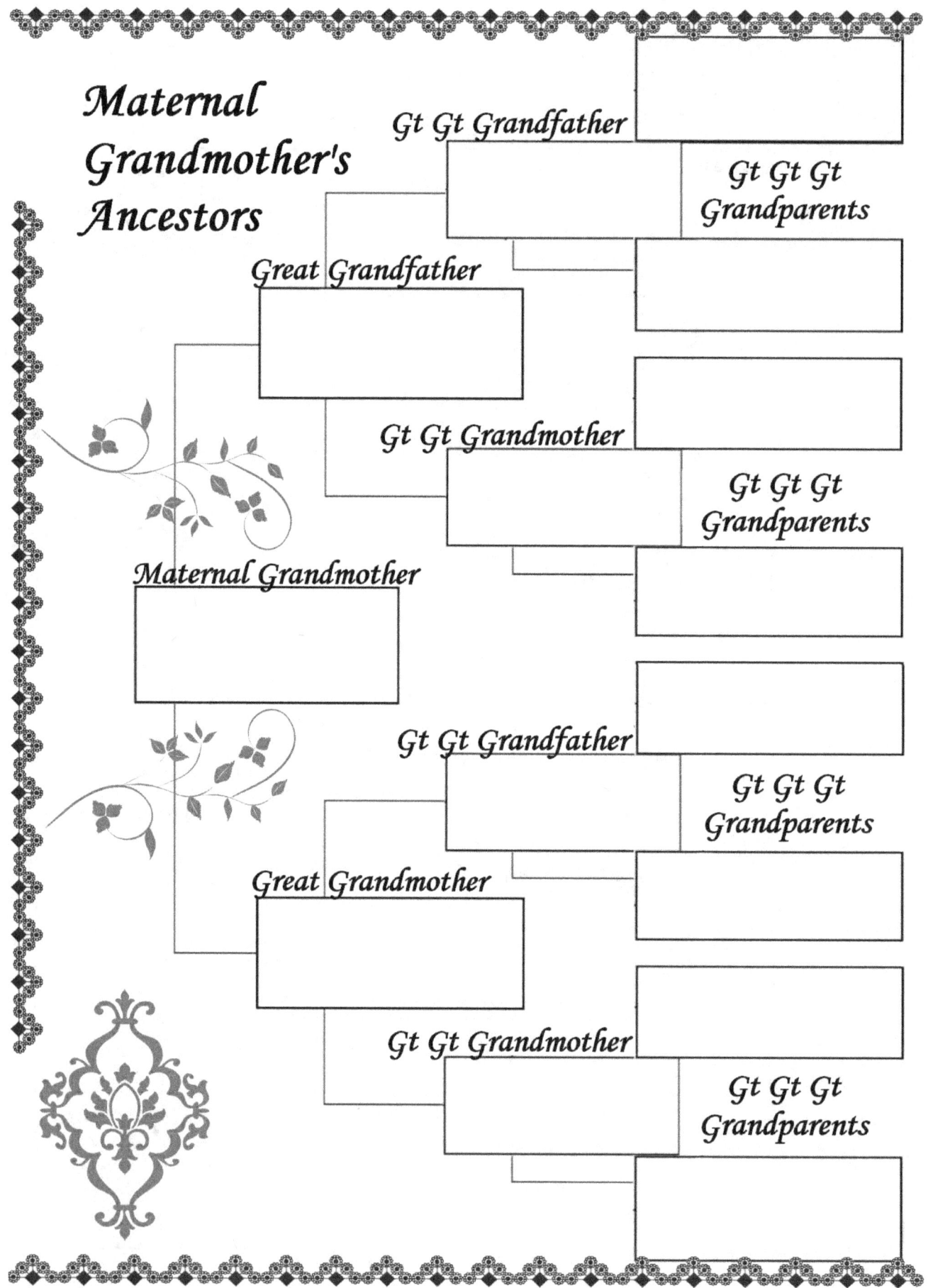

Gt Gt Grandfather

Gt Gt Gt Grandparents

Great Grandfather

Gt Gt Grandmother

Gt Gt Gt Grandparents

Maternal Grandmother

Gt Gt Grandfather

Gt Gt Gt Grandparents

Great Grandmother

Gt Gt Grandmother

Gt Gt Gt Grandparents

Child

Parents

Grandparents

Great Grandparents

Great Great Grandparents

Spouse

Spouse's Parents

Spouse's Grandparents

Spouse's Great Grandparents

Spouse's Great Great Grandparents

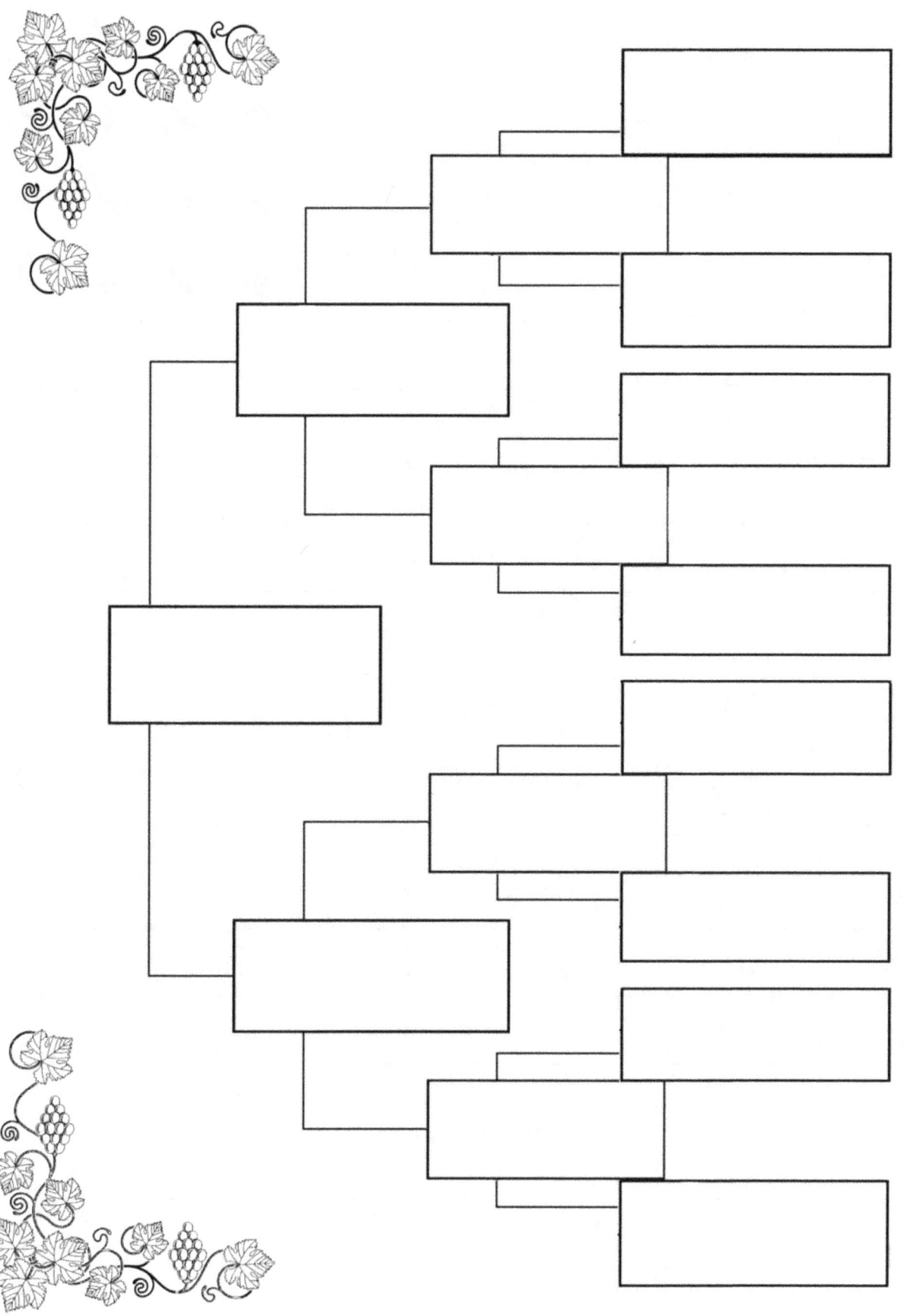

NOTES

Child

Name: _____

Born: _____

Place: _____

Spouse: _____

Married: _____

Place: _____

Parents = 2

Name: _____

Born: _____

Place: _____

Spouse: _____

Married: _____

Place: _____

Name: _____

Born: _____

Place: _____

Spouse: _____

Married: _____

Place: _____

Grandparents = 4

Name: _____

Born: _____

Place: _____

Spouse: _____

Married: _____

Place: _____

Name: _____

Born: _____

Place: _____

Spouse: _____

Married: _____

Place: _____

Name: _____

Born: _____

Place: _____

Name: _____

Born: _____

Place: _____

Spouse: _____	Spouse: _____
Married: _____	Married: _____
Place: _____	Place: _____

Great Grandparents = 8

Name:	Name:	Name:	Name:
_____	_____	_____	_____
Born:	Born:	Born:	Born:
_____	_____	_____	_____
Place:	Place:	Place:	Place:
_____	_____	_____	_____
Spouse:	Spouse:	Spouse:	Spouse:
_____	_____	_____	_____
Married:	Married:	Married:	Married:
_____	_____	_____	_____
Place:	Place:	Place:	Place:
_____	_____	_____	_____

Name:	Name:	Name:	Name:
Born:	Born:	Born:	Born:
Place:	Place:	Place:	Place:
Spouse:	Spouse:	Spouse:	Spouse:
Married:	Married:	Married:	Married:
Place:	Place:	Place:	Place:

Great Great Grandparents = 16

Name:	Name:	Name:	Name:
Born:	Born:	Born:	Born:
Place:	Place:	Place:	Place:
Spouse:	Spouse:	Spouse:	Spouse:
Married:	Married:	Married:	Married:
Place:	Place:	Place:	Place:

Name:	Name:	Name:	Name:
Born:	Born:	Born:	Born:
Place:	Place:	Place:	Place:
Spouse:	Spouse:	Spouse:	Spouse:
Married:	Married:	Married:	Married:
Place:	Place:	Place:	Place:

Name:	Name:	Name:	Name:
Born:	Born:	Born:	Born:
Place:	Place:	Place:	Place:
Spouse:	Spouse:	Spouse:	Spouse:
Married:	Married:	Married:	Married:
Place:	Place:	Place:	Place:

Name:	Name:	Name:	Name:
Born:	Born:	Born:	Born:
Place:	Place:	Place:	Place:
Spouse:	Spouse:	Spouse:	Spouse:
Married:	Married:	Married:	Married:
Place:	Place:	Place:	Place:

EXTRA CHARTS ON FOLLOWING PAGES

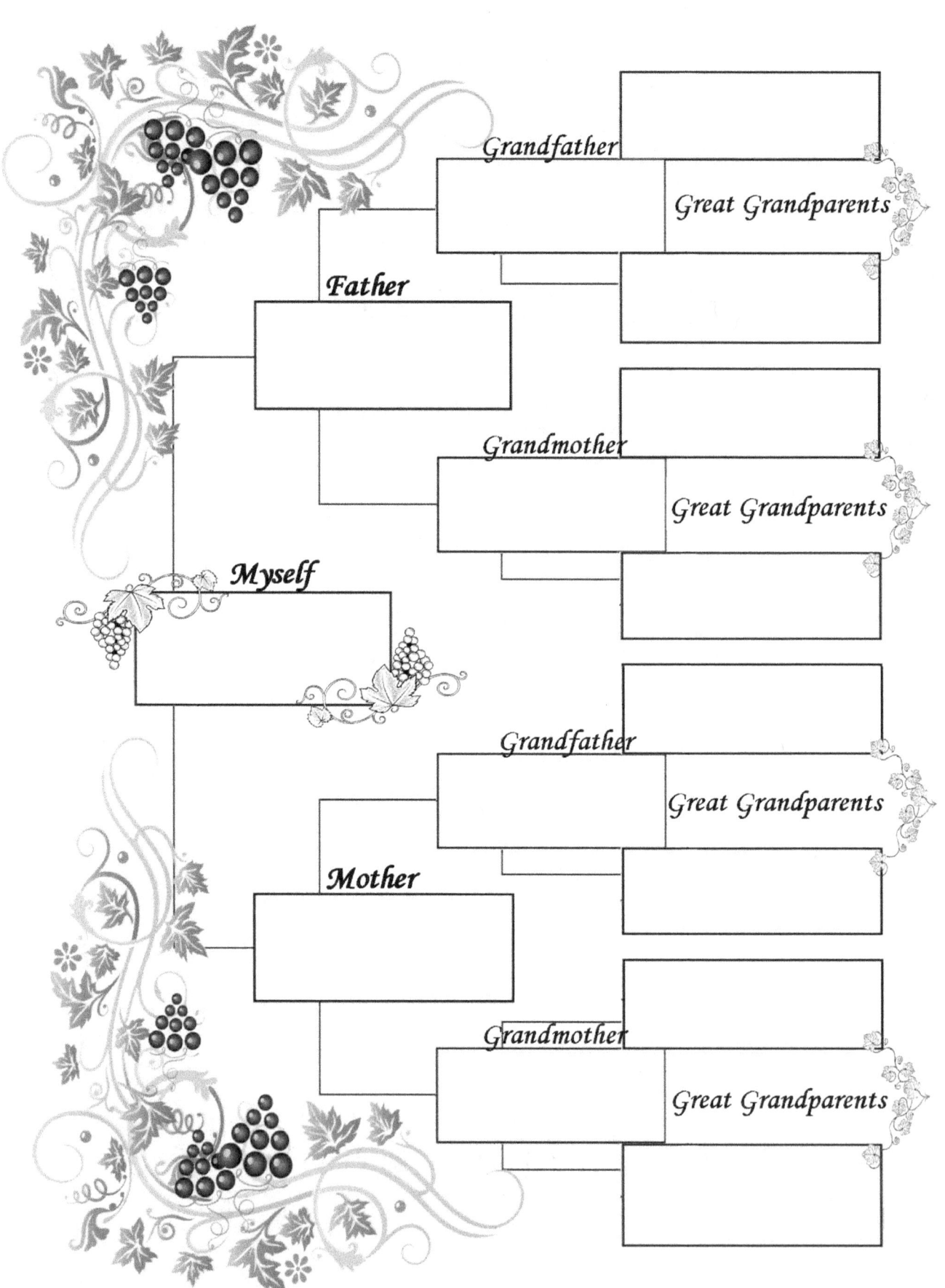

Grandfather

Great Grandparents

Father

Grandmother

Great Grandparents

Myself

Grandfather

Great Grandparents

Mother

Grandmother

Great Grandparents

Grandfather

Great Grandparents

Father

Grandmother

Great Grandparents

Myself

Grandfather

Great Grandparents

Mother

Grandmother

Great Grandparents

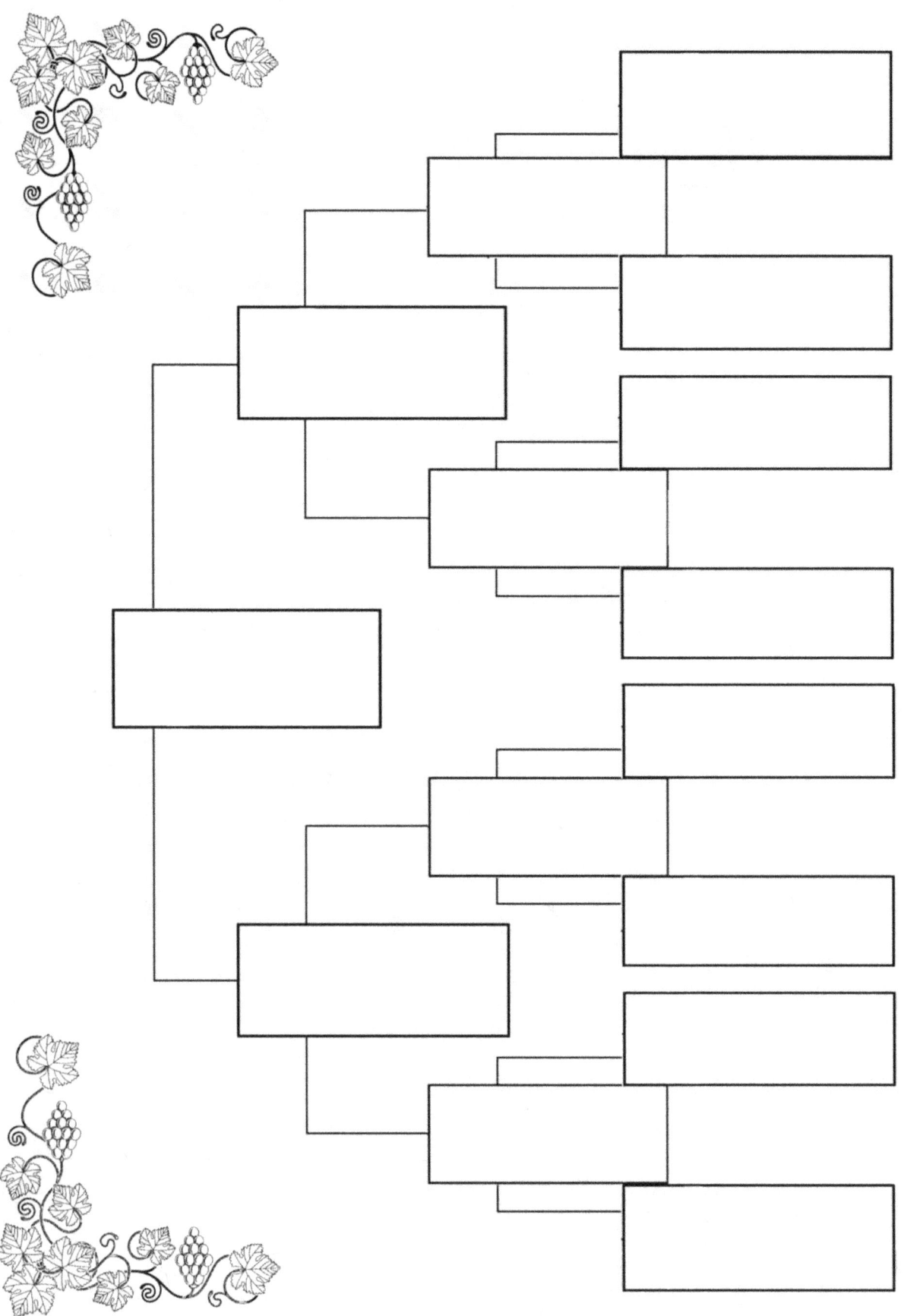

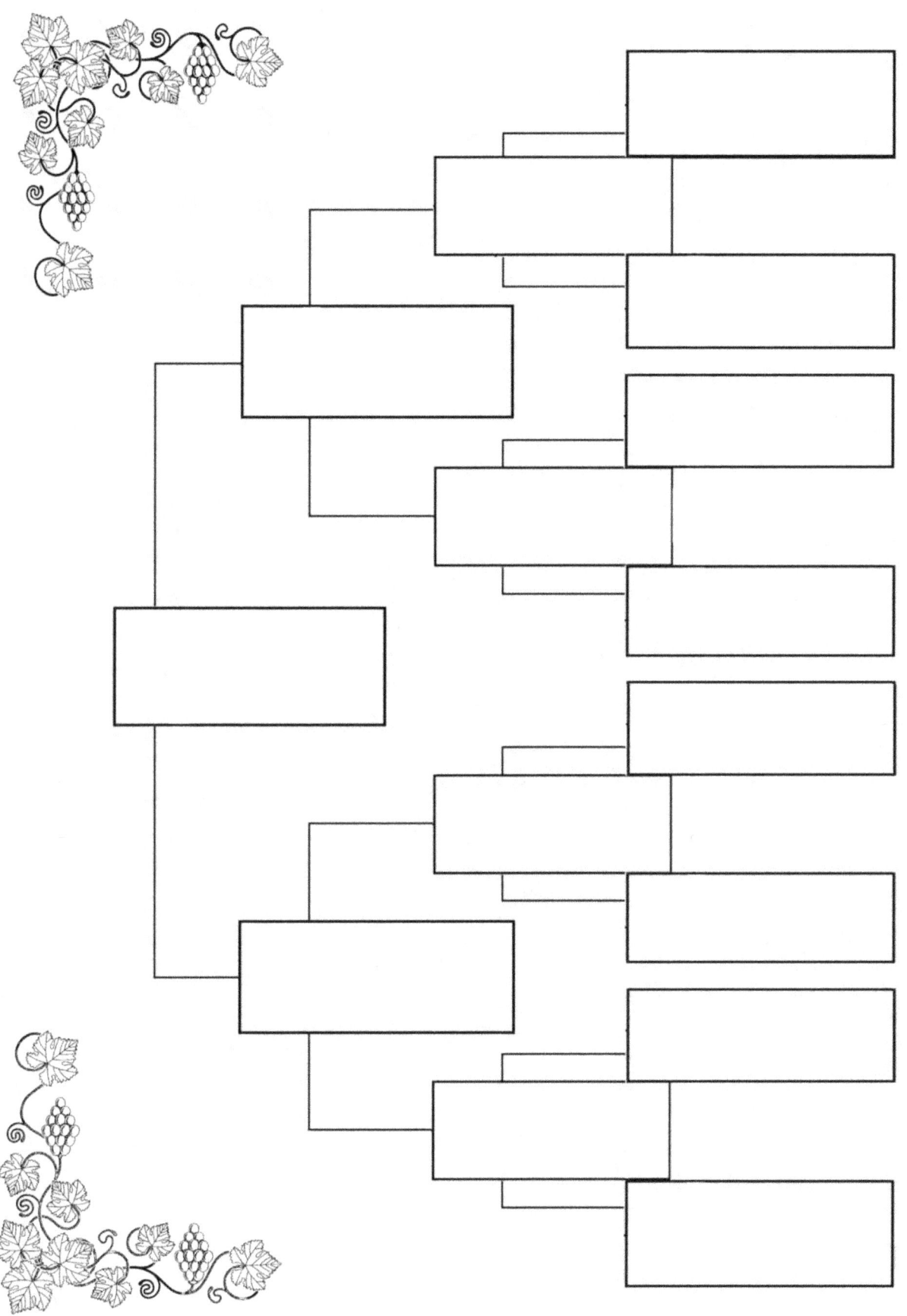